12 INCREDIBLE FACTS ABOUT THE
FIRST MOON LANDING

by Angie Smibert

12 STORY LIBRARY

www.12StoryLibrary.com

12-Story Library is an imprint of Peterson Publishing Company and Press Room Editions.

Produced for 12-Story Library by Red Line Editorial

Photographs ©: Neil A. Armstrong/NASA/AP Images, cover, 1; Bettmann/Corbis/AP Images, 4, 5, 11, 20, 21; NASA/Defense Video and Imagery Distribution System, 7, 19, 23, 24, 25, 27; NASA, 6, 8, 9, 10, 12, 13, 22, 28; Michael Collins/NASA, 14; NASA/AP Images, 15, 18, 29; Marty Lederhandler/AP Images, 17; Neil A. Armstrong/NASA, 16; Harrison Schmitt/NASA, 26

ISBN
978-1-63235-130-2 (hardcover)
978-1-63235-173-9 (paperback)
978-1-62143-225-8 (hosted ebook)

Library of Congress Control Number: 2015933666

Printed in the United States of America
Mankato, MN
June, 2015

Go beyond the book. Get free, up-to-date content on this topic at 12StoryLibrary.com.

TABLE OF CONTENTS

SPUTNIK SPARKS THE SPACE RACE

On October 4, 1957, the night sky lit up over a secret site in the Soviet Union. The Soviets had launched a missile into space. The rocket and its historic cargo reached 139 miles (223 km) above the earth. Then, the core of the rocket fell away. A shiny aluminum sphere the size of a basketball emerged. Its four long antennae unfolded. The radio transmitter inside started beeping. The world's first satellite, Sputnik 1, began to circle Earth.

Sputnik shocked the world. It fueled the fear that there was "a missile gap" between the United States and

Sputnik 1 had four long rods as its antennae.

Technicians in the Soviet Union track Sputnik's orbit.

the Soviet Union. Enemies since after World War II (1939–1945), both powers were locked in the Cold War. Each side raced to build more powerful weapons. Now Americans feared that the Soviets would use space for military purposes. President Dwight D. Eisenhower tried to downplay the feat when he congratulated the Soviets. He called Sputnik a "small ball." He then said that the United States would launch its first satellite in December.

On launch day, December 6, millions watched on TV. The US rocket rose four feet (1.2 m) off the ground. Then, it exploded. The press dubbed it "Flopnik." The United States successfully launched a satellite,

Explorer 1, on February 1, 1958. Later that year, the United States created the National Aeronautics and Space Administration (NASA). Over the next decade, the United States raced to beat the Soviet Union to the moon.

12
Years between Sputnik's launch and the first moon landing.

- The Soviet Union launched Sputnik on October 4, 1957.
- Sputnik was the first satellite.
- On February 1, 1958, the United States launched Explorer 1.

FIRE DESTROYS APOLLO 1, KILLING ITS CREW

Project Apollo would eventually lead to the first moon landing. But first, Apollo astronauts ran different tests in space to prepare.

On January 27, 1967, the Apollo 1 crew was practicing the countdown for their launch in several weeks. Their mission would be to test the Apollo Command/Service Module (CSM) in Earth's orbit. On this day, they were testing the CSM on the ground. They wanted to make sure it could run on its own power.

Astronauts Ed White, Virgil "Gus" Grissom, and Roger Chaffee entered the CSM as it sat on the launch pad. They sealed the hatch. They ran through the entire launch sequence. Six hours after they'd begun, Grissom called out, "Fire in the spacecraft!" The inside of the capsule was ablaze. The astronauts couldn't open the hatch. The outside was too hot for anyone to touch. All three astronauts died within seconds.

The Apollo 1 astronauts: Virgil "Gus" Grissom, Ed White, and Roger Chaffee

The Apollo 1 CSM after the fire

The tragic deaths delayed Project Apollo for 18 months. During that time, NASA investigated the fire. They found it was most likely started by a spark from flawed electrical wiring under Grissom's seat. They also discovered that the Apollo spacecraft was, in many ways, badly designed. The hatch couldn't be opened in under 90 seconds, for instance.

Based on the review, NASA made many changes. They redesigned the hatch. They also removed all flammable materials. More than 1,400 wiring improvements were made. After several unmanned test flights, the newly redesigned Apollo 7 launched successfully on October 11, 1968.

THINK ABOUT IT

After the Apollo 1 fire, how did NASA make the spacecraft safer? Make a list of the changes that were made.

3
Number of astronauts killed in the Apollo 1 fire.

- The astronauts were practicing for a launch.
- A fire broke out in the capsule.
- The fire may have been started by bad wiring in the cabin.
- The accident delayed Project Apollo for 18 months.
- NASA redesigned the Apollo capsule.

4

ARMSTRONG SKIPS FIRST CHANCE TO BE AN ASTRONAUT

Born in Wapakoneta, Ohio, Neil Armstrong flew navy jets during the Korean War (1950–1953).

Armstrong poses with the X-15 after a test flight.

He finished college with a degree in aerospace engineering. Then Armstrong joined the National Advisory Committee for Aeronautics (NACA) as a test pilot. One of the jets Armstrong tested was the X-15. It was a rocket-powered aircraft. It could travel beyond Earth's atmosphere.

In 1958, Armstrong was chosen for NACA's Man in Space Soonest program. The program aimed to put a man in space before the Soviet Union did. Armstrong was in the first lineup to go into space. But the program was canceled in August 1958.

In October 1958, NASA replaced NACA. The new space agency started over from scratch looking for astronauts. Armstrong was asked to apply

10

Armstrong training for the Apollo 11 mission

200

Approximate number of types of aircraft Armstrong piloted in his career.

- Armstrong didn't apply for the first group of NASA astronauts.
- He was selected for the second group of NASA astronauts, the Next Nine.
- He commanded Gemini 8 and Apollo 11.
- He was the first person to walk on the moon.

for the first NASA program—Project Mercury. But he passed. Armstrong continued to test the X-15 and other planes.

When NASA was ready to add a second group of astronauts for Projects Gemini and Apollo, Armstrong applied. In 1962, he was selected as part of NASA Group 2. It was nicknamed the Next Nine. Armstrong commanded Gemini 8 and Apollo 11. He would be the first person to walk on the moon.

SATURN V ROCKET: TALLER THAN THE STATUE OF LIBERTY

Getting to the moon required a very large rocket. On the morning of July 16, 1969, the three Apollo 11 astronauts were sitting atop of one of the largest, most powerful rockets ever made. The Apollo spacecraft included the Command Module (CM), Service Module (SM), and Lunar Module (LM). They were stacked on the rocket. With the spacecraft, the Saturn V was 363 feet (111 meters) high. That's 58 feet (18 m) taller than the Statue of Liberty.

The countdown ticked away. Inside the Apollo 11 CM, Neil Armstrong, Edwin

Saturn V launches Apollo 11.

OPERATION PAPERCLIP

Before World War II ended, the United States developed a plan called Operation Paperclip. It relocated German rocket scientists and rockets to the United States after the war. One of those scientists was Wernher von Braun. He designed the Saturn V.

"Buzz" Aldrin, and Michael Collins went over their last minute checklists. Each astronaut had a job. Armstrong was the commander of the mission.

13

Total number of Saturn V rockets that were launched.

- NASA built a family of powerful rockets for Apollo.
- Saturn V was the largest rocket.
- Saturn V took the Apollo missions to the moon.

Aldrin was the LM pilot. Collins was the CM pilot. When they reached the moon, Armstrong and Aldrin would descend to the surface in the LM. Collins would orbit in the CM. The SM contained fuel that powered the CM. It would take three days to reach the moon.

At 9:32 a.m. EDT, the Saturn V rumbled to life. It hurtled Apollo 11 into space. The Saturn V is still the largest, most powerful rocket successfully launched. And it's the only rocket to have sent humans beyond Earth's orbit.

THE EAGLE ALMOST RUNS OUT OF FUEL

On July 20, Apollo 11 made its thirteenth orbit around the moon. Aldrin and Armstrong crawled aboard the LM (nicknamed the Eagle). They undocked it from the spacecraft. "The Eagle has wings," Armstrong told NASA Mission Control in Houston.

Piloted by Collins, the CM (nicknamed Columbia) rounded the moon. The Eagle tagged along behind. "Eagle, you are go to ignite your descent engine," Mission Control told Armstrong and Aldrin. They fired the engine. The Eagle gently began its descent toward the moon.

The Eagle approached the planned landing site, the Sea of Tranquility. But Armstrong could see they were heading toward boulders. He gripped the controls and flew the Eagle manually. Armstrong peered through the triangular window at the landscape below. The Eagle kept

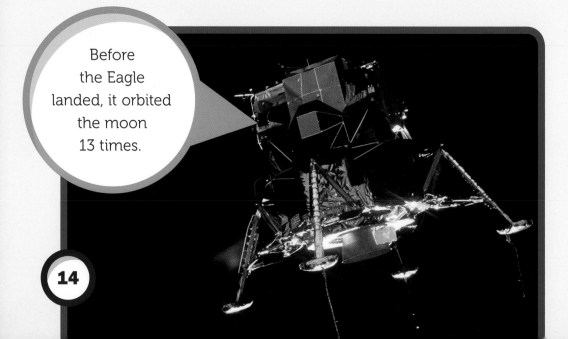

Before the Eagle landed, it orbited the moon 13 times.

descending. But he could see no place flat enough to land.

At 75 feet (23 m), Mission Control reminded Armstrong and Aldrin that they had 60 seconds of landing fuel left. But Armstrong had finally seen a place to land. "Thirty seconds," a worried Mission Control called. Ten seconds later, Armstrong touched the Eagle down. "Contact light," he reported. Then, he confirmed, "The Eagle has landed."

Mission Control in Houston, Texas, guided the astronauts to the moon.

20

Seconds of fuel left when the Eagle landed.

- The planned landing site was too rocky.
- Armstrong took manual control to land the Eagle.
- The Eagle landed in a flatter area approximately four miles (6 km) from the planned site.

HALF A BILLION PEOPLE WATCH THE FIRST MOON WALK

Armstrong backed down the ladder to the moon's surface. Before stepping off, he deployed a TV camera. This would include the world in on the moment. The camera was mounted in a compartment on the side of the LM. More than 600 million people were glued to their TV sets. In 1969, this was the largest TV audience for any event in history.

At 10:56 p.m. EDT on July 20, 1969, Americans watched as a grainy figure moved down the ladder. Then, Armstrong jumped the last three and half feet (1 m) to the surface of the moon. A moment later, Armstrong said, "That's one small step for man, one giant leap for mankind."

Aldrin joined Armstrong on the surface 19 minutes later. He described the

Aldrin walks on the moon.

moon as "magnificent desolation." For just under two hours, Armstrong and Aldrin walked—and hopped—on the moon. They collected rock samples and set up experiments. They even left mementos of fallen astronauts. From Earth, President Richard Nixon called and talked briefly to the moon walkers. The entire expedition was filmed in black-and-white. It was transmitted on live TV.

94
Percent of US households with TVs that tuned in for the moon landing.

- The two-hour moon walk was broadcast live on TV around the world.
- Armstrong was the first person to set foot on the moon.
- Aldrin walked on the moon 19 minutes after Armstrong.

People gathered in New York City's Central Park to watch the moon landing on large screens.

THE MOON SMELLS LIKE BURNED GUNPOWDER

When Aldrin and Armstrong returned to the LM after their two-hour walk on the moon, everything was covered with a fine, gray lunar dust. It clung to their spacesuits, boots, and gloves. When they took off their helmets, the astronauts noticed a new smell. The moon dust they'd tramped inside smelled like spent gunpowder.

Aldrin said the dust smelled like burned charcoal or wet fireplace ashes. But Armstrong and later astronauts agreed that it smelled like burned gunpowder. Since all of the astronauts had served in the military, they knew what gunpowder smelled like.

The astronauts left footprints on the moon's dusty surface.

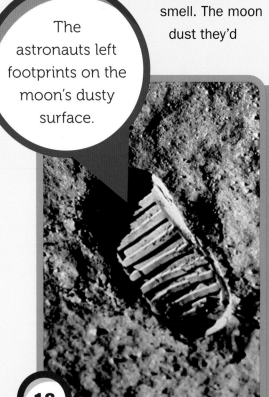

ORIGIN OF THE MOON

Before Apollo 11, no one knew how the moon was originally formed. The soil and rock samples collected by Apollo missions helped scientists make a guess. It's called the Giant Impact (or Big Splash) Theory. Approximately 4.5 billion years ago, a big space object (probably the size of Mars) hit Earth. The moon formed out of the debris of Earth and the unknown object.

A photo of the moon's surface taken during the Apollo 11 mission

2

Hours that Apollo 11 astronauts spent walking on the moon.

- Moon dust clung to everything.
- The dust smelled like burned gunpowder.
- The dust comes from meteorites smashing into the moon's surface for billions of years.

No one is quite sure why moon dust smells this way. It does not contain gunpowder. It is not flammable. If you hold a match to moon dust, nothing explodes or burns. The dust is made mostly of a type of silicon glass. The glass was formed by meteorites hitting the moon over billions of years. Each impact fused the lunar soil into glass. Then, it shattered the soil into tiny pieces. Moon dust also contains other minerals such as iron, calcium, and magnesium.

9

SOVIET PROBE CRASHES ON MOON

On July 20, 1969, something else from Earth, besides Apollo 11, landed on the moon. While Armstrong and Aldrin were collecting moon rocks, a small, unmanned Soviet spacecraft called Luna 15 began its descent. It was designed to return lunar samples to Earth. Luna 15 had launched two days before Apollo 11. It arrived in lunar orbit before the US spacecraft.

NASA discretely contacted the Soviet space agency. NASA wanted to make sure Luna 15 wouldn't interfere with the first human moon landing. It didn't. The Soviet Union agreed to keep Luna 15 in orbit longer. But

A Soviet newspaper included mention of the US moon landing on its front page.

LUNA 2

The first spacecraft on the moon wasn't Apollo 11. An unmanned Russian probe called Luna 2 landed on the moon's surface on September 12, 1959. The first American unmanned mission didn't land on the moon until 1964.

Soviet astronauts were called cosmonauts.

Luna 15 crashed when it tried to land in the Sea of Crisis.

The Soviet Union sent many more unmanned missions to the moon. But after the loss of Luna 15, the Soviet space agency gave up on human missions to the Moon. The Soviet Union began to focus its space program on building space stations instead.

15

Number of the Soviet Luna missions before Apollo 11 landed on the moon.

- Luna 15 was an unmanned spacecraft.
- It was launched by the Soviet Union.
- The spacecraft's purpose was to collect samples and return them to Earth.
- Luna 15 crashed on the surface of the moon on July 20, 1969.

THINK ABOUT IT

Why do you think the Soviet Union gave up on its plan to send a human to the moon? Write down three possibilities you come up with.

APOLLO 11 ASTRONAUTS FILL OUT CUSTOMS FORMS

After 21.5 hours on the moon, Armstrong and Aldrin lifted off in the LM. A rocket engine launched the astronauts back into orbit. They docked the LM with the CM. Then they rejoined Collins in the CM. They ejected the LM into space before heading home to Earth.

Just before dawn on July 24, 1969, the Apollo 11 CM splashed down in the Pacific Ocean west of Hawaii. Helicopters from the nearby USS *Hornet* picked up the crew and spacecraft. The chance of bringing back bacteria or viruses from the moon was slim. But the astronauts were put into decontamination suits before being flown back to the navy ship.

The three Apollo 11 astronauts wait in a raft outside the CM for a helicopter to pick them up.

3

Number of weeks the Apollo 11 astronauts spent in quarantine.

- The Apollo 11 capsule splashed down west of Hawaii.
- The USS *Hornet* picked up both capsule and crew.
- The customs forms declared they'd come from the moon.

The *Hornet* brought the astronauts to the mobile quarantine facility. This was a trailer designed to keep them separate from the public. This practice ended after Apollo 14. By then, it had become clear that the moon was lifeless.

When they reached Hawaii, the astronauts had to fill out customs forms to re-enter the United States. Anyone who travels outside the country and brings back items must fill out a customs form. Though the form may have been a joke, all three astronauts signed it. They declared the cargo to be "Moon Rock and Moon Dust Samples." And in the "departure from" blank, they wrote "the Moon." Both the CM and the quarantine trailer were then flown to Houston, Texas. The astronauts stayed in quarantine for 21 days.

The Apollo 11 crew is greeted by their wives from outside the quarantine trailer.

APOLLO 11 BRINGS BACK THREE NEW MINERALS

While on the moon, Aldrin and Armstrong collected rocks and lunar soil, or regolith. They brought them back to Earth. These samples have taught us a lot about what the moon is made of and where it came from. We now know the moon is ancient.

The rock samples date from 3.2 billion to 4.6 billion years ago. Most scientists believe Earth is a little over 4.5 billion years old.

In the samples brought back, scientists found three new minerals not then found on Earth: armalcolite, tranquillityite, and pyroxferroite. (Each of these minerals were later found on Earth, too.) Armalcolite was named after the three Apollo 11 astronauts, combining the first few letters of their last names. Tranquillityite was named after the Sea of Tranquility. These new minerals formed under high temperatures—such as in molten lava—and were then cooled rapidly.

Moon rock samples from Apollo 11 arrive at the Lunar Receiving Laboratory for study.

THINK ABOUT IT

What did Apollo 11 teach us about the moon? Find three examples from these pages to explain your answer.

This clue and many others helped scientists picture how the moon was formed. Its surface, for instance, has been melted, erupted, and crushed over billions of years. And the composition of the rocks and lunar soil shows that Earth and moon are related. They could have been formed from the same materials. Scientists are still studying the samples brought back by the Apollo missions.

47.8

Weight, in pounds (22 kg), of the moon rocks brought back by Apollo 11.

- Apollo 11 brought back samples of moon rocks and lunar soil.
- The samples taught scientists much about the origin of the moon.
- Three new minerals were discovered in the samples.

From left to right, Aldrin, Collins, and Armstrong present a moon rock to the director of the Smithsonian Institute.

NO HUMAN HAS VISITED THE MOON SINCE 1972

On December 14, 1972, astronaut Eugene Cernan left the last human footprint on the moon. As he climbed up the ladder to the LM of Apollo 17, Cernan said, "We leave as we came, and God willing, as we shall return, with peace and hope for all mankind."

By 1972, the American public was losing interest in the Apollo program. The United States was in the

Cernan salutes the flag during the last US moon landing.

12
Number of people who have walked on the moon.

- Apollo 17 was the last manned mission to the moon.
- Eugene Cernan was the last person to set foot on its surface.
- Apollo 18 and 19 were canceled.

ROBOTIC MISSIONS

Since Apollo, NASA and space agencies in some other countries have sent many robotic missions to the moon. The robots have mapped the surface, collected samples, and looked for water. They help us continue to understand the moon better.

middle of an economic recession. So NASA canceled the last planned missions—Apollo 18 and 19. NASA began planning a reusable spacecraft—the space shuttle. The space shuttle was first launched in 1981.

Even though the United States hasn't been back to the moon yet, the legacy of Apollo 11 lives on. Certainly, Apollo spurred scientific and technical advances. The United States proved that the seemingly impossible could be achieved. And Apollo 11 brought the world together, if just for a few hours, to marvel at the achievement.

Most importantly, though, Project Apollo made people look at humanity in a new way. For the first time, human beings had stood on soil that wasn't theirs. From the moon, the astronauts took photos of Earth as a whole.

People saw a pale blue marble of a world, tiny, fragile, lovely— and without borders.

A photo of Earth taken from the moon during the Apollo 11 mission

12 KEY DATES

October 4, 1957
Sputnik 1 is launched. The Space Race between the Soviet Union and the United States begins.

December 6, 1957
The first US attempt to launch a satellite into orbit fails when the rocket explodes near the ground.

February 1, 1958
The United States successfully launches a satellite, Explorer 1, into orbit.

October 1958
The National Advisory Committee for Aeronautics (NACA) is replaced by the National Aeronautics and Space Administration (NASA).

1962
Neil Armstrong is selected for the second group of NASA astronauts, the Next Nine.

September 12, 1962
President Kennedy announces his goal to put a man on the moon by the end of the 1960s.

1964
Project Gemini, a series of two-person missions in space, begins and lasts for two years.

January 27, 1967
The Apollo 1 crew is killed in a fire while practicing for a mission. Project Apollo is delayed for 18 months as changes are made to equipment.

July 16, 1969
Apollo 11 launches.

July 20, 1969
Armstrong becomes the first person to walk on the moon at 10:56 p.m. EDT. Edwin "Buzz" Aldrin follows 19 minutes later.

July 24, 1969
The Apollo 11 Command Module splashes down in the Pacific Ocean.

December 14, 1972
Astronaut Eugene Cernan is the last human to walk on the moon.

GLOSSARY

decontamination suit
Protective clothing that prevents the wearer from spreading potentially harmful substances or disease to other people, equipment, or areas.

meteorite
A meteor that reaches the surface of a planet or moon; a piece of rock or metal that has fallen to the ground from space.

missile
A weapon that is thrown, shot, or launched to strike something at a distance.

orbit
A path one body takes as it revolves around another. For example, the moon orbits Earth.

quarantine
A period during which a person with a contagious disease is isolated.

regolith
A layer of loose material that covers bedrock. The material can contain rock and mineral fragments, soil, and dust.

robotic mission
An unmanned mission; one that includes a machine that operates automatically to explore a planet, moon, or asteroid.

satellite
A machine that is launched into space and orbits Earth.

FOR MORE INFORMATION

Books

Edwards, Roberta. *Who Was Neil Armstrong?* New York: Grosset & Dunlap, 2008.

Floca, Brian. *Moonshot: The Flight of Apollo 11.* New York: Atheneum Books for Young Readers, 2009.

Mayfield, Mark. *The Spaceflight Vault: A History of NASA's Manned Missions.* Atlanta, GA: Whitman, 2010.

Yomtov, Nelson. *The Apollo 11 Moon Landing: July 20, 1969.* Chicago: Heinemann Library, 2014.

Websites

Google Moon
www.google.com/moon

NASA Education for Students
www.nasa.gov/audience/forstudents/index.html

Smithsonian National Air and Space Museum: Apollo
www.airandspace.si.edu/explore-and-learn/topics/Apollo

Student Science: The First Moon Walker
student.societyforscience.org/article/first-moon-walker

INDEX

About the Author

Angie Smibert is the author of several young adult science fiction novels, short stories, and educational titles. She was also a science writer at NASA's Kennedy Space Center for many years. She received NASA's prestigious Silver Snoopy.

READ MORE FROM 12-STORY LIBRARY

Every 12-Story Library book is available in many formats, including Amazon Kindle and Apple iBooks. For more information, visit your device's store or 12StoryLibrary.com.